American Red Cross Lifeguard Exam

"You never fail until you stop trying" - Albert Einstein

For inquiries;
info@xmprep.com

American Red Cross Lifeguard Exam #1

Test Taking Tips

☐ Take a deep breath and relax

☐ Read directions carefully

☐ Read the questions thoroughly

☐ Make sure you understand what is being asked

☐ Go over all of the choices before you answer

☐ Paraphrase the question

☐ Eliminate the options you know are wrong

☐ Check your work

☐ Think positively and do your best

Table of Contents

TEST DIRECTION

DIRECTIONS

Read the questions carefully and then choose the ONE best answer to each question.

Be sure to allocate your time carefully so you are able to complete the entire test within the testing session. You may go back and review your answers at any time.

You may use any available space in your test booklet for scratch work.

Questions in this booklet are not actual test questions but they are the samples for commonly asked questions.

This test aims to cover all topics which may appear on the actual test. However some topics may not be covered.

Studying this booklet will be preparing you for the actual test. It will not guarantee improving your test score but it will help you pass your exam on the first attempt.

Some useful tips for answering multiple choice questions;

- Start with the questions that you can easily answer.

- Underline the keywords in the question.

- Be sure to read all the choices given.

- Watch for keywords such as NOT, always, only, all, never, completely.

- Do not forget to answer every question.

1

Which of the following conditions is used to tell if a victim has a head, neck or spinal injury?

A) Unconsciousness
B) Headache
C) Severe bleeding
D) Tingling sensation in the limbs

2

Which of the following gives a correct response of the lifeguard when a patron suddenly had seizures while in the deep water?

A) Pull the patron out of the water
B) Secure the patron well onto a backboard
C) Pull the patron to shallow waters until the seizure ends
D) Keep the patron's head above the water until the seizure ends

3

A **sudden illness** can be linked to several chronic conditions like heart and lung diseases.

Which of the following does not show a symptom of sudden illness?

A) Nausea and/or vomiting
B) Impaired vision
C) Bruising of the abdomen
D) Skin complications

4

Rescue breathing is a rescue method by way of transferring air or oxygen to an unconscious and not breathing individual. It is usually done by mouth-to-mouth or an apparatus in between the two instead.

Which of the following refers to the interval of the breathing for the rescue breathing?

A) 0.5 second
B) 1 second
C) 3 seconds
D) 5 seconds

5

During CPR, what is the recommended number of chest compressions to be given for child victims?

A) 120 per minute
B) 100 per minute
C) 60 per minute
D) 40 per minute

6

Which of the following escape techniques should an individual without a life jacket do if they accidentally fall into the cold water?

A) Swim towards safety.
B) Remove all clothing and perform a survival floating.
C) Swim towards the nearest floating object and climb on it.
D) Stay warm by moving the arms and legs quickly.

7

Lifeguards can also be hired by institutions from their training facilities. The lifeguards can be made stationary or for surveillance.

Which of the following refers to the proper action of a lifeguard on surveillance duty during a busy free swim at a Cub Scout family camp?

A) Yell at the Cub Scouts who are very noisy
B) Bring rope, medicine, and bandage while roaming around
C) Carry at least two life jackets, bring telescope, and always wear your ID
D) Scan all areas in your assigned zone of coverage, wear your hip pack and carry your rescue tube with you at all times.

8

Which of the following will you consider first when fitting a life jacket?

A) Shrinkage size
B) Desired color and design
C) American Red Cross - approved
D) U.S. Coast Guard - approved

9

Which of the following is the most crucial equipment during pool emergencies?

A) Rescue tube and buoy rings
B) Backboard and AED
C) Resuscitation mask and bag-valve-mask
D) Whistle and inner tube

10

Which of the following states a situation requiring the use of a heat escape lessening position (HELP)?

A) A group of victims is awaiting rescue in cold water.
B) A victim is awaiting rescue in warm water.
C) The victim has a life jacket while awaiting rescue in cold water.
D) The victim does not have a life jacket while awaiting rescue in cold water.

11

The Department of Labor indicates the valid age and the requirements for the citizens to be able to work officially. The licensure requirements usually include age and training background.

Which of the following refers to the minimum age requirement to work as a lifeguard for swimming activities in a pool?

A) 15 years old
B) 16 years old
C) 18 years old
D) 21 years old

12

Which of the following is not avoided when caring for a victim with a suspected spine injury?

A) Performing a secondary assessment
B) Protecting the victim from colds
C) Drying the victim off and applying AED pads
D) Applying manual stabilization to the victim

13

Which of the following is the most appropriate response upon witnessing someone falling through the ice?

A) Walking out onto the ice
B) Calling 911
C) Alerting the other bystanders
D) Attempting a wading assist

14

Due to the buddy system, the lifeguards have to keep a minimum distance to their partners. A team leader or several teams can have a junior or adult leader.

Which of the following can be a good way to show respect to an adult leader when not in a surveillance duty?

A) Hide when he is present
B) Block his way and ask him how he is
C) Stand, smile, and extend your hand in the Scout handshake
D) Ask a buddy to present a dance to the adult leader

15

A **cardiac arrest** is an unexpected loss of heart function in an individual, typically with heart disease, while a **respiratory failure** is a lack of oxygen in the blood or too much carbon dioxide present in it.

Which of the following refers to the correct answer about the statement "Children typically have a cardiac arrest after they have experienced respiratory failure."?

A) The statement is true.
B) The statement is false.
C) The statement is unclear.
D) The statement is true only for some cases.

16

Lifeguards are designated for water safety and rescue. They are also in-charge of investigation of some cases or accidents that happened in the facility.

Which of the following refers to the 'F' of the FIND model?

A) Find the issue
B) Figure out the answer
C) Figure out the problem
D) Formulate questions

You, as a lifeguard, realize that one swimmer in your zone grasp his chest and submerge.

Which of the following will be the action that you should take first?

A) Use the FIND model to determine what to do
B) Scan the surroundings to see if there are other lifeguards to rescue first
C) Exercise your duty to act and perform the appropriate rescue
D) Signal the control room to send backup

Which of the following is the meaning of C in the acronym LOC?

A) Conduct
B) Compliance
C) Consciousness
D) Compression

Lifeguard training undergoes strict and rigid requirements. The hopeful passers are licensed and allowed to be employed in different swimming facilities.

Which of the following is the additional training that must be taken in order for the Lifeguard training to be valid?

A) Aquatics Administration and Life Rescue
B) Aquatics Management and Supervision
C) First Aid and CPR/AED for the Professional Rescuer
D) Safe Swim Defense and Safety Afloat

A woman complained of tingling sensations in her arms and legs after she collided with her sister on her way out of the slide. Upon inspection, the lifeguard still allowed this woman to continue swimming.

Which of the following describes the actions of the lifeguard on duty?

A) Application of the RID factor
B) Compliance to the refusal-of-care principle
C) Negligence
D) Good samaritan

21

Waterfront facilities are required by the Hazard Communication to provide a Standard Material Safety Data Sheet (MSDS) in their workplace at all times.

Which of the following can be found inside an MSDS?

A) First aid procedures and rescue equipment instructions

B) Hazards and precautions of chemicals present in the facility

C) Safety protocols during an emergency

D) Attraction and areas of the facility that require repairs

22

During surveillance, when one lifeguard is rescuing a patron in the deepwater section of a waterfront, other lifeguards on-duty should leave their position and adjust their zone coverage.

Which of the following explains the purpose of other lifeguards adjusting their zone coverage?

A) To exclude the rescuing lifeguard's zone coverage.

B) To increase the number of safety checks per area.

C) To take charge of the rescuing lifeguard's zone coverage.

D) To decrease the number of safety checks per area.

23

Which of the following can be found in an emergency action plan?

A) Emergency contacts of all participants

B) Treatment procedures of specific injuries

C) Medical insurance information

D) All of the above

24

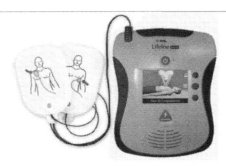

Automated external defibrillators (AED) are used to deliver electric shocks through the victim's chest to the heart.

Which of the following shows the next step after turning on an AED?

A) Apply pads to analyze the victim's heart rhythm.

B) Remind everyone to stand clear of the victim.

C) Deliver a weak electric shock to the victim.

D) Check for any signs of breathing.

CONTINUE ▶

25

Which of the following should be done to assist a disoriented victim who fell into the water?

A) Call an EMS personnel, approach and pull the victim out of the water, and follow up with additional care

B) Activate EAP, clear the pool area, and report the emergency to the management

C) Call an EMS personnel, tell the victim to swim out of the pool, and report the emergency to the management

D) Activate EAP, extend a rescue tube to the victim and follow up with additional care

26

Which of the following should be done by the lifeguard if the temperature of the lake turned cold due to the rain?

A) Warn the swimmers about the cold water and watch out for cases of hypothermia.

B) Monitor the depth of the water and ignore the water temperature.

C) Let other lifeguards warn the swimmers about the cold water.

D) Let the swimmers go straight into the cold water.

27

During a daily safety check, you noticed that several nails are sticking out from the pier.

As a life guard, which of the following should you do next?

A) Record the observations and solve the problem on a later day.

B) Immediately inform the lifeguard supervisor about the problem and suggest the restriction of the area.

C) Increase awareness to avoid possible injuries.

D) Evacuate everyone out of the lake and close the entire swimming area until the problem is solved.

28

A child was rescued after falling on the pool deck and hitting his head.

Which of the following assistance should be given if the child has a bleeding ear and complaining of dizziness?

A) Lay the child down on the deck while waiting for the arrival of an EMS staff.

B) Call for the child's parent to accompany the victim to the emergency room.

C) Assist the child in walking towards the pool office where the victim will be provided with manual stabilization.

D) Apply manual stabilization on the child's head while other lifeguards prepare the backboard.

29

Which of the following is a required skill from a shallow water lifeguard?

A) Able to recognize and respond to emergencies in pools up to 10 feet deep

B) Able to recognize and respond to emergencies in pools up to 5 feet deep

C) Able to recognize and respond to emergencies in pools up to 4 feet deep

D) Can supervise areas with diving boards, drop slides or other attractions

30

Which of the following shows an incorrect statement about sizing up an emergency scene?

A) The rescuer must wear the appropriate PPE to prevent future injuries in the scene.

B) The rescuer needs to utilize the five senses to check the safety of the scene.

C) The rescuer is required to do a primary assessment of the victim.

D) The rescuer must find out the number of victims and cause the emergency.

31

For lifeguards who are monitoring the zero-depth area of the wave pool on the roving station, which of the following should be considered?

A) Extend surveillance to total coverage when there is a large number of patrons in the pool.

B) Use a run-and-swim entry for rescue situations.

C) Assist non-swimmers in fitting their appropriate life jackets.

D) Use head and chin support for stabilizing an injured neck.

32

During a rescue situation, a resuscitation mask was already placed on a child's head in preparation for ventilation.

Which of the following will the lifeguard do next?

A) Clear up the child's airway.

B) Cover the child's mouth with the resuscitation mask.

C) Supply air by blowing into the resuscitation mask.

D) Seal the resuscitation mask.

33

Which of the following shows the best mindset for every lifeguard on-duty?

A) Everyone in the assigned zone of coverage should be monitored at all times.

B) Some cases of in-water stabilization care for head, neck, and spinal injuries may require special modifications.

C) Specialized rescue equipment should be readily accessible at all times.

D) The RID factor should always be kept in mind.

34

Accidental fecal release (AFR) refers to the introduction of stool into a swimming pool.

Which of the following is showing a correct statement about AFRs?

A) It is the concern of facility managers.

B) It is a part of the daily routine operations of the facility.

C) It must be reported to the immediately so the pool will be temporarily closed for water treatment.

D) It should be documented and shown to the media.

35

Which of the following is the most effective way of scanning an assigned zone of coverage?

A) Moving only the eyes while keeping the head still.

B) Doing a regular head count on all patrons in the zone.

C) Checking cautiously on the blind spots.

D) Moving the head and eyes around the area.

36

Which of the following is used to secure a victim suspected with a head, neck or spinal injury and prevent them from facing down at the surface of a shallow pool?

A) Arm splint technique

B) Head splint technique

C) In-line manual stabilization technique

D) Modified back support technique

CONTINUE ▶

37

Which of the following gives a correct statement?

A) Drowning ranks as the second most common unintentional deaths among children below age 15.

B) Females are four times more prone to drowning than males.

C) Children are more likely to drown in canals and ditches than in waterfront facilities.

D) There are a few cases of drowning in temperate-weather states.

38

Which of the following is the initial response when taking care of victims suffering from burns?

A) Blow air on their wound to minimize their pain

B) Give them space by keeping a distance from them

C) Remove them away from the source of the burns

D) Cool the burned area to minimize their pain

39

Which of the following shows the appropriate rescue technique for a submerged victim in a 10-feet deep pool?

A) Perform a reaching assist to help the victim resurface.

B) Use a backboard to help the victim resurface.

C) Call the attention of a trained rescuer.

D) Wear a life jacket and dive to get the victim.

40

What is the purpose of using swim classifications during a summer youth camp held in a waterfront facility?

A) To assign campers to the areas appropriate to their swimming ability.

B) To enforce a buddy system for all campers while they are in the facility.

C) To elaborate on the safety rules and regulations of the facility.

D) To pair campers with different swimming abilities.

When the number of patrons swimming in the wave pool is increasing, the waterfront facility should also increase the number of lifeguard stations for wider surveillance.

Which of the following is a correct statement?

A) This allows the lifeguard to monitor more patrons in his coverage zone.

B) This allows the lifeguards to take turns in monitoring the patrons.

C) This allows the lifeguards to take turns in patrolling the deck.

D) This allows the lifeguard to monitor less number of patrons in his coverage area.

What should a lifeguard do upon noticing a drowning victim 100 feet outside the designated swim area?

A) Alert the nearest lifeguard to rescue the victim and continue to monitor the situation.

B) Whistle for EAP and then use the available rowboat to rescue the victim.

C) Use the available backboard to perform a two-person removal from the water and then whistle for EAP.

D) Ignore other lifeguard's assigned zone of coverage.

43

Which of the following is the best way of preventing future injuries while performing surveillance on a summer youth camp?

A) Focus on the campers without life jackets.

B) Teach simple assist skills to the campers.

C) Monitor all campers in the area of responsibility.

D) Help the staff organize a swimming game for the campers.

44

Which of the following is correct for a patron complaining of neck pain and tingling sensations on both hands and feet?

A) Confirm the injury by moving the victim's head in either direction before manual stabilization is applied.

B) Confirm the injury by having the victim move his/her head in either direction before manual stabilization is applied.

C) Provide manual stabilization on the victim's head and neck and call for an EMS personnel.

D) Have the victim lie down before icing the affected area.

SECTION 1

#	Answer	Topic	Subtopic	#	Answer	Topic	Subtopic	#	Answer	Topic	Subtopic	#	Answer	Topic	Subtopic
1	D	TB	SB1	12	C	TA	SA1	23	B	TB	SB1	34	C	TA	SA1
2	D	TA	SA2	13	B	TB	SB1	24	A	TA	SA2	35	D	TA	SA1
3	C	TA	SA2	14	C	TA	SA1	25	D	TA	SA1	36	B	TA	SA1
4	B	TA	SA1	15	A	TA	SA1	26	A	TB	SB3	37	A	TB	SB1
5	B	TA	SA3	16	C	TA	SA1	27	B	TB	SB3	38	C	TA	SA2
6	C	TB	SB1	17	C	TA	SA1	28	D	TA	SA1	39	C	TB	SB1
7	D	TA	SA1	18	C	TA	SA2	29	B	TB	SB2	40	A	TB	SB3
8	D	TB	SB1	19	C	TA	SA1	30	C	TA	SA2	41	D	TB	SB4
9	B	TA	SA1	20	C	TA	SA1	31	B	TB	SB4	42	B	TB	SB3
10	C	TB	SB1	21	B	TA	SA1	32	D	TA	SA2	43	C	TB	SB3
11	A	TA	SA1	22	C	TB	SB4	33	C	TB	SB3	44	C	TB	SB2

Topics & Subtopics

Code	Description	Code	Description
SA1	Lifeguarding Skills	SB3	Waterfront Skills
SA2	Professional Rescuer and First Aid	SB4	Waterpark Skills
SA3	Cardiopulmonary Resuscitation (CPR)	TA	Lifeguarding
SB1	Basic Water Rescue	TB	Water Skills
SB2	Shallow Water Lifeguarding Skills		

CONTINUE ▶

TEST DIRECTION

DIRECTIONS

Read the questions carefully and then choose the ONE best answer to each question.

Be sure to allocate your time carefully so you are able to complete the entire test within the testing session. You may go back and review your answers at any time.

You may use any available space in your test booklet for scratch work.

Questions in this booklet are not actual test questions but they are the samples for commonly asked questions.

This test aims to cover all topics which may appear on the actual test. However some topics may not be covered.

Studying this booklet will be preparing you for the actual test. It will not guarantee improving your test score but it will help you pass your exam on the first attempt.

Some useful tips for answering multiple choice questions;

- Start with the questions that you can easily answer.

- Underline the keywords in the question.

- Be sure to read all the choices given.

- Watch for keywords such as NOT, always, only, all, never, completely.

- Do not forget to answer every question.

1

A lifeguard is assigned a buddy during his or her surveillance area and time. The designated buddy is recognized as the immediate participant that is obliged to his or her duty with the other lifeguard.

Which of the following refers to the main purpose of a buddy check?

A) Give the lifeguard a breather for other activities

B) Remind participants to remain near their buddy so they can lend assistance

C) Check the lifeguard if there are mishap in behavior

D) Assign checklists to follow when in surveillance

2

As a rescuer, which of the following will you do when a child having an asthma attack forgot to bring his inhaler?

A) Observe the victim for any changes in his condition for 20 minutes

B) Call an EMS personnel and aid the breathing of the victim by adjusting his position

C) Give 20 chest compressions to the victim

D) Borrow an inhaler from bystanders

3

Which of the following shows the dangers of alcohol intake when swimming or nearby water?

A) It can affect judgment.

B) It speeds up body movements.

C) It increases blood pressure and pulse.

D) It increases body temperature over a period of time.

CONTINUE ▶

4

Snakebites should be treated quick and calmly. It is recommended to visit the nearest hospital and get an injection of anti-venom.

Which of the following refers to the action that should be taken by a rescuer when trying to help a victim who has been bitten by a snake?

A) Chase the snake away

B) Get a stick and try to attack the snake

C) If a person is bit on the arm, elevate the arm about the level of the heart.

D) If the snake is still there, back away and approach from another direction to offer help.

5

A buddy is a partner to a lifeguard. Both are mostly together or have to check each other to confirm their status and situation.

Which of the following refers to the frequency that guards have to perform a buddy check during a recreational swim?

A) About ten minutes in between, each time

B) At the beginning and end of the recreational swim

C) Both A and B

D) Neither A nor B

6

Performing CPR may not always result in success. To be safe, immediately calling 911 will increase the possibility that life can be saved.

Which of the following refers to the three W's that a caller should follow when calling 911?

A) Who, what, where
B) When, where, who
C) Why, when, where
D) Who, when, why

7

A facility requires a lifeguard to perform his duty strictly.

Which of the following refers to the key responsibility of a lifeguard?

A) Prevent drowning and other injuries from occurring
B) Prevent entry of non-swimmers
C) Prevail in rescuing lives in the facility
D) Prepare proper reports during shifts

8

The legal considerations of a lifeguard includes his capability to act and save an individual in need. Although a lifeguard has to save the individual, he may refuse to do so if the lifeguard is not on-duty or is out of service, else, he may be liable for the consequences.

Which of the following refers to the legal consideration that immediately applies to a lifeguard in an emergency occurrence while he is performing surveillance?

A) Duty to Act
B) Duty to respond upon request
C) Informed consent
D) Ability to request a pending litigation

9

A lifesaver encounters an accident and and infant needs to be rescued. He asked for another lifeguard for safety.

Which of the following refers to the compression method to be used for two rescuers?

A) Three fingers on the sternum to deliver compressions
B) Two hands on the sternum to deliver compressions
C) Two fingers on the sternum to deliver compressions
D) One fingers on the sternum to deliver compressions

10

Infant breathing differs from adult breathing due to the difference in size. The infant is also taken care of delicately since a slight mishap can lead to further injuries.

Which of the following refer to the task that consists the infant breathing?

A) Place mouth over the nose only
B) Place mouth over the mouth only
C) Place mouth over Infant's mouth and nose
D) None of the above

11

Which of the following signs can be used to tell if a patron is suffering a head, neck, or spinal injury?

A) Headache and vomiting
B) Blurring of vision
C) Bleeding of ears and nose
D) Vomiting of blood

12

During the end of his shift, a lifeguard found a maintenance staff unconscious and not breathing. His primary assessment confirms the victim still has a pulse.

Which of the following set of actions for the situation above is arranged the correct order?

A) Activate EAP - Call an EMS staff - Provide the victim with ventilation every five seconds
B) Provide the victim with ventilation every five seconds - Activate EAP - Call an EMS staff
C) Call an EMS staff - Activate EAP - Perform CPR
D) Perform CPR - Activate EAP - Call an EMS staff

13

During an in-service training, which of the following is not included in a facility's EAP?

A) Stop the water current of the winding river.
B) Stop the wave machine via emergency stop button.
C) Stop the slide dispatch.
D) Stop anyone who exits the wave pool.

14

During a group pool visit, the facility had three lifeguards on-duty.

Which of the following cases requires emergency back-up coverage?

A) Upon activation of the facility EAP

B) When a lifeguard is not present during his/her workshift

C) When a lifeguard dives into the water to rescue a patron

D) When the number of patrons exceeds the allowed capacity of the pool

15

Hypothermia is the abnormal lowering of one's body temperature that may result in death.

Which of the following will prevent hypothermia when performing activities that require frequent submersion?

A) Taking a shower before the activities

B) Wearing multiple layers of clothing

C) Wearing a U.S. Coast Guard-approved life jacket

D) Wearing a wet suit

16

Maria was caught running on the pool deck, so the lifeguard blew the whistle to get her attention.

Which of the following steps will follow up on the enforcement of the rules and regulations?

A) Warn Maria that she has committed a violation.

B) Restrict Maria from the area.

C) Inform Maria about the possible dangers of running on the pool deck.

D) Inform Maria that she may be requested out of the facility due to her actions.

17

Which of the following describes the common problem faced by waterpark facilities?

A) Number of lifeguards and rescue equipment

B) Controlling a large number of visiting patrons

C) Variety and number of attractions/ features

D) Patrons' ignorance of the rules and regulations

18

Which of the following is correct when performing surveillance at the outer edge of a waterfront swimming area?

A) Lifeguard monitors the swimmers from an elevated position.
B) Lifeguard monitors the swimmers from a ground-level position.
C) Lifeguard monitors the swimmers from a rescue watercraft.
D) Lifeguard monitors the swimmers from a rescue tube.

19

A bleeding patron was found by lying on the ground, so an EMS personnel was called immediately. Then the lifeguard obtained the victim's consent and prepared his gloves.

Which of the following must be done next?

A) Allow the wound to stop bleeding on its own.
B) Treat the victim for shock.
C) Stop the wound from bleeding by elevating it.
D) Use a sterile dressing and bandage to press against the wound.

20

Cardiopulmonary resuscitation (CPR) consists of chest compressions and artificial ventilation done to preserve brain functions of a victim during emergencies.

Which of the following victims require a CPR?

A) A victim with airway obstruction
B) A victim with shortness of breaths
C) A victim with cardiac arrest
D) A victim with a broken leg

21

Which of the following will maintain effective patron surveillance when sun glare is affecting vision from the lifeguard station?

A) Move the lifeguard station to a position where there is no glare.
B) Discontinue the surveillance and talk to the supervisor about the problem.
C) Continue the surveillance despite the glare blocking vision in some areas.
D) Continue the surveillance when there is no more sun glare at the station.

22

Which of the following survival methods is correct when you fell in the water without a life jacket?

A) Swim towards the shore immediately.
B) Remove all clothing and perform survival floating.
C) Inflate all clothing while wearing them.
D) Remove all clothing and inflate them.

23

As a shallow water lifeguard, which of the following are your primary tasks?

A) Enforcing health codes, attending to a patron's inquiries, and encouraging patrons to shower before using the pool
B) Inspecting the pool and rescue equipment beforehand, and closely monitoring the patrons to ensure their safety inside the pool
C) Fixing the pool ropes and lane lines, and ensuring the cleanliness of dressing rooms
D) Reminding all patrons about the pool rules

24

Which of the following describes the correct follow-up procedure after a pool emergency?

A) Deal with the media.
B) Call 911 to report the incident.
C) Inspect all equipment and supplies used in the emergency.
D) All of the above

25

Which of the following is the role of a lifeguard in an emergency scene where another lifeguard is already reviving the victim via CPR?

A) Reassessing the victim
B) Providing ventilation to the victim
C) Calling for an EMS personnel
D) Assisting with the CPR

CONTINUE ▶

In an emergency, a lifeguard is sizing-up the scene, alerting the other lifeguards, performing appropriate rescue procedure, conducting a primary assessment, providing care to the victim, and then finishing with a secondary assessment.

Which of the following is true about the statement above?

A) The lifeguard is providing a demonstration during a presentation concerning safety.

B) The lifeguard is following the steps of the facility's EAP.

C) The lifeguard is in in-service training.

D) The lifeguard is preparing to provide care to a passive victim.

A swimmer in the pool is waving his hands at the lifeguard. Despite moving his arms and legs, he cannot keep his head above the water.

Which of the following is correct for the situation given above?

A) The swimmer is a passive drowning victim.

B) The distressed swimmer is in danger of drowning.

C) The swimmer is practicing his floating skills.

D) The swimmer does not need any help.

28

What will be your initial response after seeing a facility maintenance worker falling off a ladder while fixing the lightbulb of the comfort room, given the victim remained conscious?

A) Check for the victim's pulse
B) Interview the victim's current condition
C) Ask for the victim's consent to provide care
D) Provide care immediately

29

Which of the following must be done by a lifeguard when he notices a missing section of the pool gutter cover?

A) Record the observations and fix it during free time.
B) Instruct everyone to evacuate the pool and report the incidence immediately to the lifeguard supervisor.
C) Be more aware of the patrons in the pool.
D) Close the winding river until the problem is fixed.

30

Which of the following gives the appropriate action for a conscious infant who is choking?

A) Provide chest thrusts to the infant using the heels of the hand.
B) Move the infant in a position where the head is lower than the chest.z
C) Provide the infant with 10 chest thrusts and 10 back blows.
D) Put one arm around the infant's chest while standing slightly behind the victim.

31

While applying the AED pads on a victim, the rescuer noticed several jewelry are pierced on his/her chest.

Which of the following should the rescuer do next?

A) Use alcohol to wipe the chest and the jewelry.
B) Use only one pad to directly cover all the jewelry.
C) Apply the pads to the chest but not touching the jewelry.
D) Remove all the jewelry from the victim's chest.

32

Which of the following does not give a condition that may result in a head, neck, or spinal injury of patrons?

A) When deep water pools are highly supervised

B) When a patron strikes a well inflated inner tube

C) When diving is allowed in shallow pools

D) When there is a collision between patrons

33

Which of the following is the proper way of approaching a distressed patron in the swimming area when a lifeguard is aboard a motorized watercraft?

A) Approach while pointing the bow towards the victim

B) Approach from the side and turn the engine in neutral and at idle

C) Approach from downwind and down current

D) Approach quickly to assist the victim promptly

34

Which of the following considerations will ensure the effectiveness of chest compressions during CPR?

A) Allow full recoil of the chest in between compressions.

B) Perform the compressions in quick successions.

C) Place the hands at the victim's lower chest.

D) Help the victim move in a sitting position while leaning against a wall.

35

Which of the following is your initial response upon seeing a victim falling unconscious after choking on some food?

A) Look inside the victim's throat

B) Open the victim's airway

C) Apply 15 chest compressions to the victim

D) Provide ventilation to the victim

36

When planning for the safety of a group pool visit, which of the following is not important?

A) Assign the leaders and chaperones of each group

B) Ensure that there is enough lifeguards to cover all zones

C) Prepare more activities for the groups

D) Restrict anyone who goes into sections of the pool inappropriate to their swimming ability

37

A woman exiting the catch pool appears in distress so the facility's EAP was activated.

Which of the following must be done after extending a rescue tube towards her?

A) Pull the woman to safety and call the medical team for additional care.

B) File a report about the incident and discuss it with bystanders.

C) File a report about the incident and discuss it with the media.

D) Pull the woman to safety and inspect the rescue tube.

38

A child who slipped on the deck is conscious but is suspected of a head, neck or spine injury.

Which of the following should the lifeguard consider when providing care to the victim?

A) Secondary assessment should not be performed.

B) Immediately provide the necessary care even without checking the scene.

C) Manual stabilization can be provided even without the victim's consent.

D) The victim should not be moved unless there is an incoming danger.

39

Which of the following holds a correct statement about the huddle position?

A) It is provided to two or more persons with life jackets floating in cold water.

B) It is provided to children and elderly persons in the water.

C) It is provided to three or more persons without life jackets floating in cold water.

D) It is provided to a single person without a life jacket floating in cold water.

CONTINUE ▶

40

An adult was rescued by the lifeguard beside the speed slide. This patron is unable to sit up and is having tingling sensations in his toes, feet, and legs.

Which of the following should the lifeguard do next?

A) Offer help to the patron and conduct a secondary assessment upon his consent.

B) Advise the patron to rest and closely monitor his condition.

C) The patron is expected to have a head, neck or spinal injury so apply medical attention as needed.

D) Ask other lifeguards to conduct a safety check on the slide.

41

Which of the following shows an important preparation for aquatic emergencies?

A) Enforce the use of goggles and swimming fins.

B) Determine the potential hazards of the surroundings.

C) Participate in all recreational water activities.

D) Contact the U.S. Coast Guard for the history of past accidents.

What kind of assistance would you give to victims in shallow water who are suspected of a head, neck or spinal injury?

A) For conscious victims, assist them out the water and stabilize their necks.

B) For unconscious victims, perform the hip and shoulder support.

C) Call 911 and request the help of another lifeguard.

D) Turn the victims face up and perform the head-splint technique.

Which of the following is a correct way of performing a reaching assist with a rescue tube when rescuing a child near the side of the pool?

A) Extend a rescue tube to the child and tell them to swim to safety.

B) Extend a rescue tube to the child and pull them to safety.

C) Kneel on a pool deck, extend a ring buoy to the child and pull them to safety.

D) Swim towards the child and slide them onto a backboard.

CONTINUE ▶

A lifeguard noticed a distressed patron at the deepest area of a crowded wave pool.

Which of the following shows the correct procedure for rescuing the patron?

A) Activate the EAP, alert the other lifeguards about the situation, and throw a ring buoy to the patron

B) Enter cautiously onto the trough of the next wave, rescue the patron immediately, and ask for other lifeguard's assistance

C) Activate the EAP, wait for the wave to stop, and perform the appropriate rescue

D) Activate the EAP, enter cautiously onto the crest of the next wave using a compact jump, and perform the appropriate rescue

SECTION 2

#	Answer	Topic	Subtopic	#	Answer	Topic	Subtopic	#	Answer	Topic	Subtopic	#	Answer	Topic	Subtopic
1	B	TA	SA1	12	A	TA	SA2	23	B	TB	SB2	34	A	TA	SA3
2	B	TA	SA2	13	D	TB	SB4	24	D	TB	SB1	35	B	TA	SA2
3	A	TB	SB1	14	C	TA	SA1	25	C	TA	SA2	36	C	TA	SA1
4	D	TA	SA1	15	D	TB	SB1	26	B	TB	SB2	37	A	TB	SB4
5	C	TA	SA1	16	C	TA	SA1	27	B	TB	SB2	38	D	TA	SA1
6	A	TA	SA1	17	C	TB	SB4	28	C	TA	SA2	39	A	TB	SB1
7	A	TA	SA1	18	C	TB	SB3	29	B	TB	SB2	40	C	TB	SB4
8	A	TA	SA1	19	D	TA	SA2	30	B	TA	SA2	41	B	TB	SB1
9	C	TA	SA1	20	C	TA	SA3	31	C	TA	SA2	42	C	TB	SB1
10	C	TA	SA1	21	A	TA	SA1	32	A	TA	SA1	43	B	TB	SB2
11	C	TA	SA1	22	C	TB	SB1	33	C	TB	SB3	44	D	TB	SB4

Topics & Subtopics

Code	Description	Code	Description
SA1	Lifeguarding Skills	SB3	Waterfront Skills
SA2	Professional Rescuer and First Aid	SB4	Waterpark Skills
SA3	Cardiopulmonary Resuscitation (CPR)	TA	Lifeguarding
SB1	Basic Water Rescue	TB	Water Skills
SB2	Shallow Water Lifeguarding Skills		

CONTINUE ▶

TEST DIRECTION

DIRECTIONS

Read the questions carefully and then choose the ONE best answer to each question.

Be sure to allocate your time carefully so you are able to complete the entire test within the testing session. You may go back and review your answers at any time.

You may use any available space in your test booklet for scratch work.

Questions in this booklet are not actual test questions but they are the samples for commonly asked questions.

This test aims to cover all topics which may appear on the actual test. However some topics may not be covered.

Studying this booklet will be preparing you for the actual test. It will not guarantee improving your test score but it will help you pass your exam on the first attempt.

Some useful tips for answering multiple choice questions;

- Start with the questions that you can easily answer.

- Underline the keywords in the question.

- Be sure to read all the choices given.

- Watch for keywords such as NOT, always, only, all, never, completely.

- Do not forget to answer every question.

1

The signs of a heart attack must be recognized to prevent it. If the event cannot be prevented, call 911 immediately and prepare lifesaving treatment.

Which of the following hold true for the statement 'Sharp, stabbing twinges of pain in the chest is a sure sign of a heart attack'?

A) The statement is true.

B) The statement is unclear.

C) The statement is false.

D) The statement is neither true nor false.

2

The manager decided to have one lifeguard for patron surveillance for one day at the waterfront facility.

Which of the following is a correct generalization about the lifeguard?

A) He/She is responsible for total coverage.

B) He/She will serve as back-up coverage.

C) He/She is responsible for zone coverage.

D) He/She will be assigned to several lifeguard stations.

3

A victim who is not breathing requires proper lifesaving measure. Calling 911 and acting on one's capabilities should be one of the first things that you should do.

Which of the following should be done if you see a child collapsed on the floor without breathing signs?

A) Activate EMS

B) Wait for an ambulance

C) Start CPR immediately

D) Let the child wake up naturally

4

Which of the following equipment must always be accessible to the lifeguard on-duty?

A) Mask, snorkel, and fins

B) Whistle, rescue tube, and resuscitation mask

C) Gloves, resuscitation mask, and an automated external defibrillator

D) Rescue tube, gloves, and emergency oxygen

CONTINUE ▶

5

A lifeguard activates the facility's EAP the dives into the water to rescue a submerged victim.

Which of the following shows the role of other lifeguards on the scene?

A) Continue monitoring the assigned zone of coverage.

B) Assisting on pulling the victim to safety and preparing the backboard for the victim.

C) Collecting a document of witness accounts and controlling the crowd.

D) Reporting the incident to the manager and calling for an ambulance.

6

National Camp Standards (NCS) is a standard used to ensure the quality of the trainees according to the basic quality, including capability and age, to obtain such training and complete it.

Which of the following refers to the age requirement for serving as a lifeguard in swimming activities according to NCS?

A) 12 years old

B) 14 years old

C) 16 years old

D) 18 years old

7

Figure out the problem
Identify possible solutions
N....
Determine the best solution

A lifeguard acronym FIND is given above. What does the letter "N" in the FIND model remind you to do?

A) Name the pros and cons

B) Nullify the circumstances

C) Negate the adverse effects

D) Notify the lifeguard supervisor

8

Which of the following shows the next step in a primary assessment after checking the scene?

A) Checking the victim for responses

B) Checking the victim's pulse

C) Calling an EMS personnel

D) Clearing up the victim's airway

9

A woman who has been swimming in laps went missing for a while after she dived underwater. The lifeguard noticed that she had not resurfaced yet.

Which of the followingis correct about the woman's situation?

A) She is a passive victim who needs help.

B) She is an active victim who needs help.

C) She is an experienced swimmer who does not need help.

D) She is a distressed swimmer who needs help.

10

Non-swimmers can enjoy the pool in the depths that can be above shoulder or less. To ensure safety, they must declare this upon entry.

Which of the following refers to the action that non-swimmer Scouts should do?

A) Be encouraged to suit up and join in the testing

B) Be given a chance to play and splash in the water

C) Both A and B

D) Neither A nor B

11

Which of the following strategies can be used to prevent injuries during a summer youth camp?

A) The RID factor

B) Buddy pairs

C) Back-up coverage

D) A and B

12

Which of the following is true for a swimmer who is floating face-down in the water, his or her arms are still, and he or she is not breathing?

A) The swimmer is distressed.

B) The swimmer is holding his or her breath.

C) The swimmer is a struggling drowning victim.

D) The swimmer is a passive drowning victim.

13

Which of the following is described as the monitoring of the patrons in the pool and checking the bottom, middle and the surface of the pool?

A) Patrolling

B) Effective scanning

C) Guarding

D) Conducting safety check

14

Swimming on turbid water will require the swimmer to swim no more than 8 meters away from shore. It is necessary that the swimmer is visible from the lifehouse.

Which of the following is the primary action if you observe a person fails to surface after submersion in murky water?

A) Immediately undertake a rescue attempt

B) Wait for the proper equipment to start rescue

C) Call your buddy and start a meeting for an action plan

D) Wait for 5 minutes before attempting rescue

15

For victims who fell in warm water without a life jacket, which of the following must they do while waiting for help?

A) Perform scissor kicks to tread water

B) Perform breaststrokes to prevent overheating

C) Perform a survival floating

D) Perform crawl strokes with your head above the water

16

A lifeguard is recommended to take charge of safety or water rescue in a swimming facility. The open water and close water areas are defined according to their depth, size, and clearness.

Which of the following defines turbid water according to the Safe Swim Defense?

A) A small white ball not visible in 2 feet deep water

B) A 12-inch white disk is not visible 3 feet underwater

C) A swimmer treading water cannot see his feet

D) The bottom area is not clear

CONTINUE ▶

A heart attack victim should be taken care of immediately. In a life-threatening situation, call 911 then start the lifesaving procedure.

Which of the following holds for the statement, "The best treatment for all heart attack victims is immediate CPR."?

A) The statement is unclear.
B) The statement is false.
C) The statement is true.
D) The statement is false only for some cases.

Which of the following describes a safety check procedure done in most waterpark facilities?

A) Checking unusual noises and fixing missing pieces or mildewed safety netting
B) Checking the height restrictions before allowing a patron to an attraction
C) Patrolling the grounds to assist lost children
D) Posting rules and closing the attractions

19

Which of the following gives a correct statement about general waterpark rules?

A) Rules may not be posted anywhere in the facility as long as they are announced at a public address system.

B) Rules must be short and concise for the swimmers to read them easily.

C) Rules must be posted on the changing rooms so everyone can see them.

D) Rules must be detailed and posted near every attraction in the facility.

20

Which of the following statements about manual in-line stabilization of victims with suspected head, neck or spinal injury is correct?

A) It can be provided by bystanders when the lifeguard is occupied in clearing the pool.

B) It is provided using the head-splint technique.

C) It is less important than on land stabilization technique.

D) It can only be performed with the supervision of an EMS personnel.

21

Which of the following describes the correct way of launching a rescue board?

A) Climb behind the middle of the board and lie down.

B) Straddle the end of the board and sit still.

C) Hold the board high up in the air until the water reaches waist level.

D) Lay the board on the shoreline and push it forward.

22

Which of the following must be your response when an automated external defibrillator (AED) requires you to give a shock to the victim?

A) Cover the AED pads with a blanket.

B) Start with chest compressions.

C) Apply new pads to the victim's chest.

D) Keep everyone distant from the victim.

23

Which of the following conditions requires a shallow water lifeguard to have total coverage surveillance inside the facility?

A) Only one diving board is available.

B) The winding river where adults are walking has a water current.

C) The lap pool has a varying depth from 5 feet to 10 feet.

D) All of the above

24

Which of the following ventilation equipment offers the best protection against any disease transmission?

A) CPR breathing barriers

B) AED pads

C) Disposable nitrile gloves

D) Rescue tube

25

Which of the following methods would best reduce the number of injuries and accidents in a pool?

A) Monitor the performance of other lifeguards.

B) Scan the assigned pool area and relieve them from any hazards.

C) Remind all patrons about the pool rules and regulations.

D) All of the above

26

Which of the following involves recognizing a distressed swimmer, rescuing an active victim, informing the management and speaking with a witness?

A) In-service training

B) Emergency action plan

C) Communication plan

D) Emergency rescue plan

27

Which of the following is the alternative rescue technique for a distressed swimmer in the edge of the pool when a reaching equipment is unavailable?

A) Beach drag technique
B) Extend arms from the deck and grasp the victim
C) Approach and pull the victim in the arms
D) Throw a ring buoy to the victim

28

Which of the following shows an effective way of scanning an area of wave pool from a nearby lifeguard station?

A) Count all the patrons in the area of responsibility.
B) Move only the head and eyes to scan the area of responsibility.
C) Be more conscious about blind spots inside the facility.
D) Stare at a fixed direction.

29

A lifeguard is about to perform a deep-water line search to rescue a submerged patron.

Which of the following methods will provide the lifeguard with more vision and let him cover more distance with less effort?

A) Asking other patrons to participate in the search
B) Using extra oars and paddles
C) Using a watercraft
D) Wearing mask and fins

30

You were separated from your team, and you accidentally fell through the ice.

Which of the following techniques will help you survive?

A) Reach for the edge of the ice to pull yourself up then roll away from the broken ice.
B) Move out of the ice by using a breaststroke kick and roll away from the broken ice.
C) Move out of the ice by using a strong kick, stand and return to shore.
D) Perform a survival floating.

31

If you saw a woman got injured but still has not lost consciousness, which of the following will you do?

A) Provide the necessary medical care immediately to the woman.

B) Ask for the woman's consent first before checking for any life-threatening conditions and interview her about the incident.

C) Check for any life-threatening conditions and interview her about the incident.

D) Assist the woman to the nearest first aid station, ask for her consent and then providing her with the necessary medical care.

32

Which of the following is the most important task of a lifeguard?

A) Conduct a brief orientation about the pool rules.

B) Fix the pool ropes and lane lines as well as maintain the cleanliness of changing rooms.

C) Inspect all areas of the pool and check the availability of rescue equipment before the opening of the facility

D) Attend to patron's inquiries and ensures that they take a shower before swimming.

33

From a nearby station, the lifeguard noticed a male adult who is swimming across the pool underwater.

Which of the following is the most correct course of action?

A) Call the patron using a whistle and then escort him to leave the pool

B) Document the violation and show it to the manager after the shift

C) Stop the patron immediately then explain the dangers of his actions

D) Activate the EAP, clear the pool then escort the patron out of the pool

34

Which of the following terms is described as the setting of multiple lifeguard stations to reduce the number of swimmers watched by each lifeguard?

A) Set coverage

B) Total coverage

C) Multiple coverage

D) Zone coverage

35

Cardiac Chain of Survival is described as the chain of events done rapidly in successions to cardiac arrest victims to maximize the chances reviving them.

Which of the following is done first in a Cardiac Chain of Survival?

A) CPR

B) Defibrillation

C) Advanced medical care

D) Recognition and access to the EMS

36

Which of the following guidelines ensures the general water safety of everyone in performing activities near or in the water?

A) Learn the basic procedures during emergencies.

B) Learn boating, first aid, and CPR skills.

C) Wear a U.S. Coast Guard-approved life jacket.

D) All of the above

37

Which of the following shows the correct position of the hands when giving chest compressions to an infant?

A) One hand is on the chin; the other is on the chest.

B) One hand is on the forehead; the other is on the chest.

C) One hand is on the chin; 2-3 fingers of the other hand is on the center of the chest.

D) One hand is on the forehead; 2-3 fingers of the other hand is on the center of the chest.

38

Several people were injured after the bleachers during a swim meet suddenly collapsed.

As the lifeguard on duty, who among the following victims would you provide with care first?

A) Child with a broken arm

B) Unconscious woman

C) Mother with a crying infant

D) Child with a slightly bleeding cut in his leg

Which of the following gives the correct location of the fists when performing abdominal thrusts to an adult?

A) On the rib cage
B) In the middle of the abdomen
C) In the middle of the breastbone
D) In the lower part of the abdomen

Which of the following actions is needed when a dispatch lifeguard noticed a loose handrail of the pool slide?

A) Temporarily restrict the access to the slide after ensuring everyone has had their turn.
B) Temporarily restrict the access to the slide immediately and inform the lifeguard supervisor.
C) Write a comprehensive report about the findings and talk to the media.
D) Fix the problem on a later day when no one is using the slide.

Which of the following escape technique is advisable when your vehicle is sinking after it plunged into the water?

A) Exit through an undamaged door before water enters the vehicle
B) Exit through the vehicle door when the vehicle is about half full of water
C) Roll up all windows to prevent water entry then exit through the door when the vehicle settles
D) Exit out of a window when the vehicle is nearly full of water

As a lifeguard, you noticed that an adult patron collided with a child patron on his way out of the slide, so both patrons got submerged in the water.

Which of the following should be your most accurate response to the situation above?

A) Expect the child to have injuries in the head, neck, or spine.
B) Activate the EAP immediately, retrieve the backboard and ask for other lifeguard's assistance.
C) Activate the EAP immediately and perform a multiple victim rescue.
D) Monitor the victims for possible injuries before taking any actions.

The lifeguard found a facility staff lying unconscious on her back next to a ladder. Upon primary assessment, the victim was still breathing.

Which of the following shows the next best step before requesting for help?

A) Adjusting the victim into H.A.IN.E.S position
B) Using clothes to pull the victim into an open area
C) Activating the facility EAP
D) Scanning the victim for possible injuries

A part of the waterfront facility has been temporarily closed due to a large amount of debris in the water.

Which of the following must be the next best step by the lifeguard?

A) Announce to everyone the hazards present in that area and install warning signs and buoys as a safety reminder.
B) Announce to everyone the hazards present in that area upon noticing swimmers trying to go to that area.
C) Expect other lifeguards to announce to everyone the hazards present in that area.
D) Move the lifeguard station away from the city.

SECTION 3

#	Answer	Topic	Subtopic	#	Answer	Topic	Subtopic	#	Answer	Topic	Subtopic	#	Answer	Topic	Subtopic
1	C	TA	SA1	12	D	TB	SB1	23	B	TB	SB2	34	D	TA	SA1
2	A	TA	SA1	13	B	TA	SA1	24	A	TA	SA2	35	D	TA	SA2
3	A	TA	SA1	14	A	TB	SB1	25	B	TB	SB2	36	D	TB	SB1
4	A	TB	SB3	15	C	TB	SB1	26	B	TA	SA1	37	D	TA	SA2
5	B	TA	SA1	16	C	TB	SB2	27	B	TB	SB1	38	B	TA	SA2
6	C	TB	SB1	17	B	TA	SA1	28	A	TB	SB4	39	B	TA	SA2
7	A	TA	SA1	18	A	TB	SB4	29	D	TB	SB3	40	B	TB	SB4
8	A	TA	SA2	19	D	TB	SB4	30	B	TB	SB1	41	D	TB	SB1
9	A	TA	SA1	20	B	TA	SA1	31	B	TA	SA2	42	A	TB	SB4
10	C	TB	SB1	21	A	TB	SB3	32	C	TA	SA1	43	A	TA	SA1
11	B	TB	SB3	22	D	TA	SA2	33	C	TA	SA1	44	A	TB	SB3

Topics & Subtopics

Code	Description	Code	Description
SA1	Lifeguarding Skills	SB3	Waterfront Skills
SA2	Professional Rescuer and First Aid	SB4	Waterpark Skills
SB1	Basic Water Rescue	TA	Lifeguarding
SB2	Shallow Water Lifeguarding Skills	TB	Water Skills

CONTINUE ▶

TEST DIRECTION

DIRECTIONS

Read the questions carefully and then choose the ONE best answer to each question.

Be sure to allocate your time carefully so you are able to complete the entire test within the testing session. You may go back and review your answers at any time.

You may use any available space in your test booklet for scratch work.

Questions in this booklet are not actual test questions but they are the samples for commonly asked questions.

This test aims to cover all topics which may appear on the actual test. However some topics may not be covered.

Studying this booklet will be preparing you for the actual test. It will not guarantee improving your test score but it will help you pass your exam on the first attempt.

Some useful tips for answering multiple choice questions;

- Start with the questions that you can easily answer.

- Underline the keywords in the question.

- Be sure to read all the choices given.

- Watch for keywords such as NOT, always, only, all, never, completely.

- Do not forget to answer every question.

1

Which of the following situations does not allow a beach drag rescue technique?

A) Scene is a shallow, sloping beach

B) Only one rescuer is available

C) Victim is possibly injured in the head, neck or spine

D) Victim is heavier than the rescuer

2

When providing care to a heart attack victim, which of the following will you consider doing first?

A) Check the victim for any life-threatening conditions.

B) Open the victim's airways.

C) Loosen the victim's clothes.

D) Call for an EMS personnel.

3

Who among the following victims requires the assistance of an EMS personnel?

A) A woman with intermittent abdominal pressure

B) A child with a lightly bleeding cut on his hands

C) A woman with airway obstruction

D) A child with an open leg wound and a protruded bone

4

An **Emergency Action Plan**, or EAP for short, is a standard procedure for lifeguards during rescue and lifesaving. It is necessary that the procedures be followed to ensure the safety and life of the victim.

Which of the following refers to the first step after applying in-line stabilization and determining that the victim is not breathing?

A) Maintain stabilizing the victim and ensure ventilation

B) Remove the victim from water and let him stay beside the pool

C) Remove the victim from the water and start planning the next step

D) Remove the victim from the water using the Extrication Using a Backboard at the Pool Edge technique

CONTINUE ▶

5

Which of the following is the interval between successive resuscitation mask ventilation of a 7-year-old child?

A) 2 seconds

B) 5 seconds

C) 7 seconds

D) 8 seconds

6

During emergency cases, it is important to follow the standard safety and rescue procedures. The emergency also needs to be available upon request.

Which of the following refers to the skills to be used with a face-down victim who has a suspected spinal injury in waist-to-chest-deep water?

A) Head splint

B) Head and chin support

C) Neither A not B

D) Either A or B

7

What is the first priority of rescuers when assisting a victim during an emergency?

A) Calling the attention of an EMS personnel

B) Checking for responses from the victim

C) Sizing up the scene

D) Immediately providing care without or without the victims' consent

8

Which of the following refers to the step that is taken after a successful rescue?

A) A report is filled out by the lifeguard

B) A report is filled out by the victim

C) A report is filled out by the ambulance team

D) A report is filled out by the camping advisor

9

Which of the following methods is correct when a lifeguard is surveilling during a busy family swim session?

A) Always have a first aid kit, an AED and a backboard nearby at all times.

B) Always have a rescue tube nearby at all times.

C) Focus on the blind spots of the facility.

D) Restrict all areas with a water depth over 5-feet.

10

Which of the following explains the purpose of a secondary assessment during emergencies?

A) To scan the area for unseen victims that might need medical attention

B) To identify and address the non-life threatening conditions of the victims

C) To the medical insurance number of the victim

D) To check if there is severe bleeding on the victim

11

A person is floating in the surface water that is 4ft deep and appears to be unconscious. Considering your job, as a lifeguard, the most natural thing is to approach and rescue the person.

Which of the following techniques should be used to rescue the individual?

A) Passive victim front rescue

B) Slow swim approach

C) Active rescue

D) Submerging rescue

12

Which of the following describes the recommended depth of the chest while performing compressions on an adult?

A) 1.5 inches or more

B) At least 1 inch

C) At least 0.5 inch

D) 2-2.5 inches

13

Which of the following describes the appropriate position of the victim while performing head-splint inside a wave pool?

A) Head is upstream

B) Head is same level as the heart

C) Feet is upstream

D) Feet is facing away from the waves

14

Upon rescuing an injured swimmer, he is usually placed beside the pool. If there is no EMS personnel in the area, the victim will not be moved unnecessarily.

Which of the following refers to the case where the victim has to be moved?

A) When there are people who wants to move the victim

B) When you need to treat some minor cuts

C) When they are in danger where they are

D) None of the above

15

On the event of a water rescue, the rescuing lifeguard will serve as the main rescuer while the support lifeguard will remain as the assisting responder.

If the rescuing lifeguard has used a head-splint to help stabilize a subject with suspected spinal injury, which of the following refers to the action to be taken by the assisting responder after placing the backboard under the subject?

A) Remain on deck and take over stabilization

B) Move the victim over to another back board

C) Shout for help and visit the director's office

D) Secure the subject's head using a head immobilizer

16

Which of the following rescue techniques will you use for a victim who is having a seizure in the water?

A) Place a spoon between the victim's teeth.

B) Grab and hold the victim still in the water.

C) Grab and keep the victim's head and face above the water.

D) Grab and pull the victim out of the water.

17

For waterpark lifeguards, which of the following should be readily available to them throughout their duty?

A) Rescue tubes, gloves, and resuscitation mask

B) Radio, whistle, and resuscitation mask

C) PPEs, emergency oxygen, and manual suction device

D) PPEs, rescue tubes, and first aid kits

18

The RID Factor is assumed to be the leading causes of why drowning occurs.

Which of the following refers to the 'I' in the RID Factor?

A) Intrusion

B) Isolation

C) Irritation

D) Implementation

19

A lost swimmer search is a type of activated search that reports the swimmer to be lost while swimming in the area. A team of lifeguards can be the first person to start the search.

Which of the following refers to the equipment used by lifeguards in the lost swimmer search?

A) Wear lifejackets

B) Use floating devices

C) Wear a mask and fins

D) Include two more teams for a search

20

If a conscious victim is saved, it is necessary to call the ambulance still to check for further internal injuries. The necessary procedure may entail hospitalization or out-patient visit.

Which of the following refers to the action not to be taken after removing a responsive victim with a suspected spinal injury from the water?

A) Keep the victim's temperature at normal levels

B) Loosen the chest strap and apply the pads of an AE

C) Talk to the victim and reassure him about his condition

D) Double check that EMS Rescue was called and on the way

21

Which of the following is the main task of lifeguards in waterfront facilities?

A) Enforcing the facility's rules and regulations

B) Monitoring the other lifeguards on duty

C) Completing daily records and reports in time

D) Opening/closing attractions and performing safety checks

22

During a family outing in a waterfront facility, a 5-year old choked on some food.

After a rescuer was given the consent of the child's family, which of the following should be done next?

A) Perform 30 chest compression and then 2 ventilations

B) Perform 20 chest compression and then 2 ventilations

C) Perform 3 back blows and 3 abdominal thrusts from behind of the victim

D) Perform 5 back blows and 5 abdominal thrusts from behind of the victim

23

The cloudy and turbid water will spell danger to swimmers, especially for wide beaches. Even if there are many lifeguards on duty, the difficulty of life rescue rises due to the water conditions.

Which of the following refers to the activities prohibited on turbid waters?

A) Surfing

B) Team building

C) Run-and-dive entry

D) Diving and underwater swimming

24

The principal responsibility of a lifeguard is to prevent accidents and injuries happening in the swimming facility. So, it is necessary that a lifeguard is quick to respond to emergencies.

Which of the following is the recommended time to be able to reach the furthest part of a lifeguard's designated area according to the CDC Model Aquatic Health Code?

A) 15 seconds

B) 30 seconds

C) 45 seconds

D) 1 minute

25

Which of the following shows the best way of protecting oneself from possible bloodborne pathogen transmission when providing care to victims?

A) Use dressings and bandages as barriers during contact.

B) Wash the hands thoroughly and use hand sanitizers before and after contact.

C) Interview the victim for any history of communicable diseases before contact.

D) Wear disposable gloves and mask before contact.

26

Which of the following is the appropriate cycle of chest compressions and ventilation for infants?

A) 10; 3

B) 15; 2

C) 15; 3

D) 10; 2

27

SAMPLE is an acronym for the interview questions when asking a patient about his/her brief history.

What does the A in the acronym stand for?

A) Age

B) Affiliation

C) Allergies

D) Academy

28

In a waterfront facility, which of the following gives the correct response during a weather-related power failure?

A) Evacuate everyone out of the pools and into safety.

B) Allow the swimmers inside the pool but warn them about the power failure.

C) Let the swimmers stay on the sides of the pool and their feet dipped in the water.

D) Allow the swimmers inside the pool while staying alert on weather updates.

29

Safe Swim Defense is a required skill or technique that provides steps and ability to participate in activities involving swimming safely. It is a requirement before you can join sports and water rescue.

Which of the following refers to the fitness evidence required by the Safe Swim Defense plan?

A) Signed health history form
B) Signed waiver for acidents
C) Signed document for liability
D) Signed parent consent

30

Which of the following gives the correct description for an emergency medical services (EMS) system?

A) It is a network of community resources that provides care during emergencies.
B) It is a set of simple and easy-to-remember steps during emergencies.
C) It is used to prevent emergencies in, on and around the water.
D) It is used to report hazards in an emergency.

31

Which of the following would you do to help a woman who fell off her inner tube while exiting a catch pool?

A) Use a reaching pole to pull her to safety.

B) Reach across the rescue tube, grasp her on the armpit and help her stand up.

C) Throw a rescue tube that she can use to swim to safety.

D) Lift her out of the water and onto the side of the deck after resting the rescue tube under her knees.

32

Which of the following must be considered by the lifeguard when monitoring a busy family swim session?

A) Have an available first aid kit, AED, and backboard nearby.

B) Monitor areas in the coverage zone with a readily accessible rescue tube nearby.

C) Restrict entry in pools with a water depth of over 5-feet.

D) Prepare a life jacket for each patron in the coverage zone.

33

While on surveillance, a lifeguard noticed that high winds are creating large waves and blurring vision at the waterfront facility.

Which of the following is the most proper action from the lifeguard?

A) Evacuate everyone out of the waterfront and lead them into safety.

B) Restrict everyone from going beyond the edge of the floating platform while their feet is in the water.

C) Allow everyone to stay in the waterfront but stay tuned for incoming weather reports.

D) Allow everyone to go into the water.

34

Which of the following can decrease the risk of AED pads touching each other when dealing with a small child or an infant?

A) Put one pad on the chest while the other is on the back.

B) Put one pad on the stomach while the other is on the chest.

C) AED pads are not advisable on a small child or an infant.

D) Put the pads on the chest such that they are in reverse positions.

35

The lifeguard on the area noticed that a distressed patron suddenly went under water.

Which of the following is the correct response to the scenario above?

A) Act fast and perform the appropriate rescue for the victim.

B) Alert the other lifeguards to provide care for the victim.

C) Perform the necessary actions based on the RID factor.

D) Scan the area while waiting for the emergency back-up coverage.

36

Which of the following strategies is prohibited when performing surveillance on a waterfront facility?

A) Classify swimmers and designate them to appropriate areas based on their swimming abilities.

B) Pair swimmers and instruct them to check on their partner from time to time.

C) Always be alert of the water and weather conditions.

D) Lead the swimmers out of the facility for periodic safety checks.

37

Suppose you are assisting a victim with a suspected spinal injury, which of the following is the correct way of strapping the victim on a backboard?

A) Head first, then upper chest, then hands, and lastly thighs

B) Feet first, then thighs, then arms, and lastly head

C) Hands first, then legs, and lastly upper chest

D) Upper chest first, then hips, and lastly thighs

38

An unconscious patron who was rescued out of the pool was infrequently gasping. Using a primary assessment, the presence of a pulse from the victim was confirmed.

Which of the following gives the next best step by the lifeguard?

A) Checking the victim for severe bleeding

B) Monitoring the victim's breathing patterns

C) Performing CPR on the victim

D) Providing the victim with 2 ventilation

CONTINUE ▶

39

Which of the following does not give a primary responsibility of the facility management?

A) Conducting staff seminars and in-training
B) Addressing the attractions/features that require repairs
C) Establishing and revising policies and procedures
D) Enforcing and educating patrons about the rules and regulations

40

Musculoskeletal injuries are the soft tissue injuries caused by a sudden impact, force, vibration, and unbalanced positions to the muscles, nerves, ligaments, joints, blood vessels, neck, and lower back.

When assisting a victim with musculoskeletal injury, what is the correct meaning of the acronym RICE?

A) Rest, immobilize, cold, elevate
B) Remove, ice, care, evaluate
C) Remove, immobilize, cold, evaluate
D) Rest, ice, care, elevate

41

Which of the following describes the best sequence of actions when rescuing a motionless victim in the water?

A) Perform primary assessment - activate EAP - call an EMS personnel - perform secondary assessment - size up the scene
B) Size up the scene - activate EAP - call an EMS personnel - perform primary assessment - perform secondary assessment
C) Activate EAP - dive into the water - perform the appropriate rescue, move the victim to safe exit point - remove the victim from the water - provide emergency care as needed
D) Perform secondary assessment - perform primary assessment - size up the scene - activate EAP - call an EMS personnel

42

You are suspecting that the victim submerged underwater has a head, neck or spinal injury.

Which of the following should be considered when providing care to this victim?

A) Prevent movement of the victim's head and neck using the head-splint technique.

B) Prevent movement of the victim's head and neck using the head hold technique.

C) Rescue the victim out of the water while preventing movement of his head and neck.

D) Quickly transfer the victim onto a backboard without moving his head and neck.

43

Which of the following is correct about a lifeguard's cooperation with other lifeguards, staff, and supervisors of the facility?

A) Team cooperation is the task of facility management.

B) Team cooperation is a primary responsibility of a lifeguard.

C) Team cooperation should be the main discussion during in-service meetings and hiring orientations.

D) Team cooperation is included in the facility's EAP.

44

A bag valve mask (BVM) is hand-held medical equipment used in providing positive pressure ventilation to victims with difficulty in breathing or is not breathing at all.

Which of the following shows a correct statement about BVMs?

A) They are readily available in all emergencies.

B) It is not required to monitor the full exhalation of the victim.

C) They are operated by two rescuers.

D) They are used by a single rescuer.

SECTION 4

#	Answer	Topic	Subtopic	#	Answer	Topic	Subtopic	#	Answer	Topic	Subtopic	#	Answer	Topic	Subtopic
1	C	TB	SB1	12	C	TA	SA2	23	D	TB	SB2	34	A	TA	SA2
2	D	TA	SA2	13	A	TB	SB1	24	B	TB	SB1	35	A	TA	SA1
3	D	TA	SA2	14	C	TB	SB1	25	D	TA	SA2	36	D	TB	SB3
4	D	TB	SB1	15	A	TB	SB1	26	B	TA	SA2	37	D	TA	SA1
5	C	TA	SA2	16	C	TB	SB1	27	C	TA	SA2	38	D	TA	SA2
6	D	TB	SB2	17	A	TB	SB4	28	A	TA	SA1	39	D	TA	SA1
7	C	TA	SA2	18	A	TB	SB1	29	A	TB	SB2	40	A	TA	SA2
8	A	TB	SB1	19	C	TB	SB2	30	A	TB	SB1	41	C	TA	SA1
9	B	TA	SA1	20	B	TB	SB1	31	B	TB	SB2	42	A	TA	SA1
10	B	TA	SA2	21	A	TA	SA1	32	B	TA	SA1	43	B	TA	SA1
11	A	TB	SB2	22	D	TA	SA2	33	A	TB	SB3	44	C	TA	SA2

Topics & Subtopics

Code	Description	Code	Description
SA1	Lifeguarding Skills	SB3	Waterfront Skills
SA2	Professional Rescuer and First Aid	SB4	Waterpark Skills
SB1	Basic Water Rescue	TA	Lifeguarding
SB2	Shallow Water Lifeguarding Skills	TB	Water Skills

TEST DIRECTION

DIRECTIONS

Read the questions carefully and then choose the ONE best answer to each question.

Be sure to allocate your time carefully so you are able to complete the entire test within the testing session. You may go back and review your answers at any time.

You may use any available space in your test booklet for scratch work.

Questions in this booklet are not actual test questions but they are the samples for commonly asked questions.

This test aims to cover all topics which may appear on the actual test. However some topics may not be covered.

Studying this booklet will be preparing you for the actual test. It will not guarantee improving your test score but it will help you pass your exam on the first attempt.

Some useful tips for answering multiple choice questions;

- Start with the questions that you can easily answer.

- Underline the keywords in the question.

- Be sure to read all the choices given.

- Watch for keywords such as NOT, always, only, all, never, completely.

- Do not forget to answer every question.

1

Waterfront areas are prone to strong winds and waves. It is also susceptible to bad weather conditions like thunder and heavy rains.

Which of the following actions should be taken first when a thunderstorm threatens an outside aquatics area?

A) At the first sound of thunder, clear the pool

B) Call the weather station to confirm the weather conditions

C) Wait for the second sound of thunder then evacuate

D) Run as far as possible to avoid the storm

2

Basic Life Support is a support system that is dedicated to lifesaving. This procedure may include the use of AED and CPR.

Which of the following are the initial Basic Life Support (BLS) steps for adults?

A) Assess the individual, activate EMS and get AED, check pulse, and start CPR

B) Assess the individual, check pulse, activate EMS and get AED, and start CPR

C) Start CPR, get AED, activate EMS, asses the individual

D) Start CPR, activate EMS, operate the AED, check the rhythm

3

Hypothermia refers to the body condition of a patient when the heat of the body is continuously lost. The body becomes cold and may lead to death.

Which of the following refers to the cases which increases the risk of hypothermia?

A) Old age

B) Intake of alcohol

C) Both A and B

D) None of the above

4

Breathing refers to the action of the lungs, providing oxygen to the body, while the pulse refers to the heart rhythm, the heart's tactile arterial palpation.

Which of the following holds true for the statement "Breathing and pulse tasks can be checked simultaneously"?

A) The statement is true.

B) The statement is false.

C) The statement is unclear.

D) The statement is true only for some cases.

CONTINUE ▶

5

A buddy may be far away even when you need him.

Which of the following refers to the action that must be taken if your buddy takes over 10 seconds to respond to you?

A) Scold him for being lazy

B) Act on his behalf and do it solo

C) Report him to the administrative office

D) Remind him of his responsibility for the other's safety.

6

An **in-line stabilization technique** is a technique used by a second individual that is responsible for applying counter-movement for the patient. It is necessary that suspected head, neck, or spine injuries be stabilized immediately.

Which of the following refers to the in-line stabilization technique that should be used when placing a responsive victim with a suspected head, neck or spinal injury on a backboard?

A) The over-arm head splint

B) Head support

C) Chin and spine support

D) Standing posture

7

With the presence of advanced airway in an adult victim, the CPR and life rescue will improve. The advance airway apparatus helps stabilize the breathing of the victim during the CPR.

Which of the following refers to the frequency breaths administered during two-rescuer CPR?

A) Every 1 to 3 seconds (20-30 breaths per minute)

B) Every 3 to 6 seconds (10-20 breaths per minute)

C) Every 6 to 8 seconds (7 to 10 breaths per minute)

D) Every 8 to 10 seconds (6-7 breaths per minute)

8

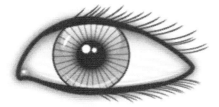

Eye injuries are one of the most difficult to treat in an emergency. Calling 911 will help you take care of it.

Which of the following hold true when treating an eye injury?

A) Use distilled water to rinse the eye
B) Roll your eyes to remove foreign object
C) Irrigate chemical contamination in the eye for 10 minutes
D) If an object penetrates the eye, you should bandage or tape the object in place and call EMS

9

Lifeguards are usually in a team of two's and three's. Areas near floating play structures are to be inspected at all times for the safety of the swimmers.

Which of the following refers to the degrees of overall views that a team should apply?

A) 60 degrees
B) 90 degrees
C) 360 degrees
D) 270 degrees

10

Swimmers are classified according to the depth that they can handle. Non-swimmers usually stay at 5ft and can swim around 10m while swimmers can stay at deeper levels and swim longer distances.

Which of the following is the distance required for the Swimmer swim classification?

A) 50 feet
B) 100 yards
C) 50 yards
D) 100 feet

11

Heat exhaustion is the body condition when a patient's body is overheated. Some people may directly collapse due to the severity of the condition.

Which of the following refers to the symptoms and signs that may occur in patients with heat exhaustion?

A) Sweating
B) Chilling
C) Confusion
D) None of the above

12

An event that requires the pool to be fully occupied will have to be reported before being accepted by the management. The lack of lifeguards may result in an issue or accident if not handled correctly.

Which of the following refers to the type of coverage that is used by setting up multiple lifeguard stations?

A) Total Coverage
B) Zone Coverage
C) Partial Coverage
D) Conservative Coverage

13

During swimming marathons, lifeguards are recommended to be present to ensure the safe and sound finish of the event.

Which of the following set-up should lifeguards have during the event?

A) Rowboats with three occupants accompanying each swimmer
B) Rowboats with two occupants accompanying each swimmer
C) Lifeguards in anchored rowboats 100 yards apart along the course
D) Lifeguards in anchored rowboats guard 2 swimmers in a distance

14

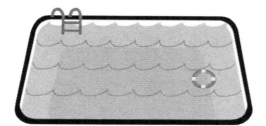

The safety of the area is assigned to an individual or a team of lifeguards. The area of coverage depends on the safety standards set by the affiliated organization and the safety inspection unit.

Which of the following refers to the individual or team that is responsible for the identification of potential hazards on or around the swim area?

A) Lifeguards
B) Team leader
C) Aquatics supervisor
D) All of the above

15

An infant CPR must be differentiated from an adult CPR. An infant may need more delicate care while an adult may be subject to a more rigid procedure.

Which of the following is to be used when performing a CPR for an infant?

A) A palm
B) 2 palms
C) 2 fingers
D) AED

16

Some swimming facilities do not have the lifeguards available. This is due to the minimal requirement for the lifeguards or the place being a training facility instead.

Which of the following is the minimum rescuer-to-swimmer ratio for a recreational swim unit when there is no presence of professional lifeguards in the facility under Safe Swim Defense?

A) One guard for every 3 participants
B) One guard for every 10 participants
C) One guard for every 13 participants
D) No guards are needed

17

CPR, or Cardiopulmonary Resuscitation, is a method for lifesaving. It is mostly used for unconscious and not breathing victims.

Which of the following refers to the components of a CPR?

A) Airway

B) Breathing

C) Chest compressions

D) All of the above.

18

The water temperature is essential to the swimmers to prepare necessary swim clothing in case it is too cold or too hot. The lifeguard is also responsible for the dissemination of information.

Which of the following action would be proper after the lifeguard confirmed that the water is cold due to a recent storm?

A) Tell the swimmers that the cold can be disregarded

B) Do not emphasize that the cold water can affect their swimming activity

C) Alert swimmers to the cold water and watch for signs of hypothermia

D) Let the swimmers discover the temperature them tell them more information

CONTINUE ▶

19

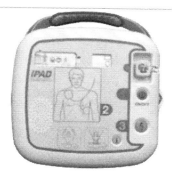

An AED, or **Automated External Defibrillator**, is an external device that is portable and hand-carried. It is used to deliver an electric current and stop the arrhythmia.

Which of the following refers to the use of an adult AED towards a child?

A) It can be used.

B) It cannot be used.

C) It can be used for 5 yrs old and above.

D) It cannot be used because it will overheat.

20

Chest compression involves a technique in order for it to be performed well. You have to be adequately trained so that the basic mistakes when doing a CPR can be avoided.

Which of the following is the next step that you have to do after each compression?

A) Check the pulse

B) Allow the chest to recoil

C) Give another rescue breath

D) Follow another compression immediately

21

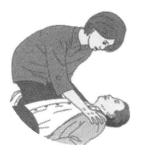

Response

While walking with a friend, you, as a lifeguard, see a child collapsed in the ground. The child is unconscious without breathing signs, and you have to start CPR.

Which of the following refers to the most necessary thing that your friend should do to help you while you start rescuing the victim?

A) Check the child's airway

B) Activate the emergency response system

C) Help you perform CPR immediately

D) Let your friend help activate your lifesaving app

22

Chest compressions will serve as the preliminary step in CPR to pump air to the lungs and recover its function asap.

Which of the following refers to the number of standard compressions in a minute?

A) 80-100 compressions

B) 100-120 compressions

C) 120-150 compressions

D) 150-180 compressions

CONTINUE ▶

23

A **lookout** is usually a person responsible for scouting the area, especially beaches and large swimming pools, to ensure safety and prevent drowning. Most of the time, the lookouts are the ones responsible for communicating with the personal below the station.

Which of the following refers to the preliminary responsibilities of a lookout according to Safe Swim Defense?

A) Call for buddy checks every 5 minutes, operate the buddy board, guard the gate

B) Hang life tags onboard, buddy check each and every time, guard the gate

C) Supervise other lookout, check person incharge, open gates

D) Monitor the weather, alert rescue personnel, identify violations of Safe Swim Defense

24

A head or neck injury in the water may directly result in drowning. Lifeguards are supposed to be able to organize rescue in a short amount of time to avoid further complications.

Which of the following refers to proper manual in-line stabilization with regards to a head or neck injury?

A) It cannot be used in water rescue

B) It can only be used in water rescue

C) It is the only technique needed if EMS rescuers are present

D) It is provided using the head splint technique

25

Some facilities allow disabled individuals to swim and enjoy the pool. It is necessary that the individual is capable of being in the water.

Which of the following refers to the action to be done if a disabled person wants to check-in for a recreational swim with his friend?

A) Allow them to swim in the area that matches their ability
B) Report them for disobeying the facility rules
C) Disallow them to enter the facility
D) Allow them to hire personal lifeguard first

26

The beginner area on a waterpark is reserved for those who are not comfortable to tackle the deeper pools. It is usually recommended that beginners should stay in the beginner area.

Which of the following refers to the maximum depth of the beginner area?

A) Just over the head
B) Waist level
C) Should level
D) Head level

27

The American Heart Association is an organization that cares for heart surgeries and injuries. At the same time it disseminates information for cardiac arrest and heart illness prevention.

According to the 2015 AHA guidelines, which of the following are the recommended sequence of steps for CPR?

A) Chest compressions, Airway, Breathing
B) Airway, Breathing, Check pulse
C) Both A and B
D) Neither A or B

28

AED usage will require technical staff to perform it. The medical response team will have the required personnel to operate it.

Which of the following refers to an act that is not recommended when using an AED?

A) After a shock is delivered, allow 10 seconds before resuming CPR.
B) Check the pulse before continuing with compressions after a shock.
C) Do not place on medication patches.
D) Make sure the area around the person is clear.

29

Model Aquatic Health Code (MAHC) is a relative manual that is endorsed towards lifeguards and water rescuers for the advanced and scientific approach of life rescue. It is made a standard in today's age to be able to apply for the post of a lifeguard in a swimming pool or waterpark.

Which of the following refers to the time frame given to a lifeguard to reach the furthest zone of the pool according to MAHC?

A) 2 minutes
B) 1 minute
C) 45 seconds
D) 30 seconds

30

First aid is given to primarily stop the bleeding or preventing further injuries to the patient. First aid can be given by trained personnel in the area.

Which of the following refers to the definition of first aid?

A) The first help given to a victim
B) A treatment for the victim's worry
C) The professional treatment given to a victim
D) A prescrption medicine that helps stabilize the victim

31

As a lifeguard, communication is a vital key to saving lives. The importance of the relay of communication can either result in death or the safety of life.

Which of the following is the necessary response you can do to facilitate communication with an adult leader while on surveillance duty?

A) Request to leave the post

B) Suggest to come back later

C) Allow a third person to witness the conversation

D) Stand and make eye contact with the adult

32

Large scale open water resorts require lifeguards to be on patrol. They are usually in speedboats or other floatable devices capable of carrying a rescued victim.

Which of the following refers to the assisting approach that is used for a struggling victim who is in a considerable distance to be reached in a very short time?

A) Rowing assist

B) Throwing assist

C) Shouting assist

D) Pulling assist

CONTINUE ▶

Harmful insects are called parasites. They infest a person and give him harm while purposefully benefitting from him.

Which of the following refers to the insect that is almost invisible, burrows into the skin and causes itching?

A) Common lice
B) Chigger
C) Wood tick
D) Spotted Tick

Some insects contain pollen and allergen. They carry these while roaming around and searching for food.

Which of the following refers to the condition when an allergy occurs due to an insect bite?

A) Epileptic shock
B) Emotional shock
C) Fainting
D) Anaphylactic shock

35

Natural nose bleeding occurs when a person's nasal membranes dry up and crack. The bleeding will stop in time, but it is better to cure it and prevent further bleeding.

Which of the following refers to the treatment of a nose bleed?

A) Apply pressure on the nose and head, apply cold compress

B) Lean the head back, wipe the blood, apply cold compress

C) Have the victim lean forward, apply gentle pressure on the nostril, apply cold towels

D) Squeeze the nostrils, wipe the blood, apply cold compress

36

A first-degree burn is a burn classification that refers to the burning of the epidermis. This causes slight pain and redness.

Which of the following refers to the treatment of first-degree burns?

A) Apply burn ointment.
B) Wrap the burnt area in soft cloth.
C) Wash the burnt area with soap and warm water.
D) Apply cool running water until there is little or no remaining pain.

37

A lookout is a person that is liable for overseeing the swimming platform or facility. Usually, a lookout is designated to a specific range or area in the facility to avoid a mishap.

Which of the following serves as the minimum qualification in order to be a lookout under the Safe Swim Defense Plan?

A) 1st class underwater training
B) Sound understanding of Safe Swim Defense
C) Training in CPR and lifesaving
D) Currently trained lifeguard

Good samaritan law is a law precisely targeted at protecting individuals triying to help or asist individuals who are injured or in danger.

Which of the following refers to the fear that keeps most people from attempting CPR?

A) The fear of not being paid

B) The fear of being unrecognized

C) The fear of not having appropriate assitance

D) The fear of doing CPR incorrectly and hurting the patient.

A **lifeguard** is a type of rescue personnel, situated in beaches or swimming pools. They are incharge of the safety of the swimmers and the participants in water sports and activities.

Which of the following refers to the primary responsibility of a lifeguard?

A) Prevent fist fights and quarrels

B) Ensure that there is no illicit activities in the area

C) Prevent drowning and other injuries from occurring

D) Communicate with other lifeguards to maintain communication

40

During compressions, it is necessary to stop for a while so that the chest would be able to rise. You can start the next compression after this step.

Which of the following should be checked if the chest of a patient does not rise during the breathing task?

A) Eyes

B) Pulse

C) Nose

D) Airway

41

Chest compressions and rescue breathing mainly comprise the basic CPR procedure. The standard steps must be followed to avoid any delay in rescue and lifesaving.

Which of the following is the critical characteristics of high-quality CPR?

A) Pushing hard and fast

B) Minimizing interruptions between compressions

C) Starting chest compressions within 10 seconds of recognition of cardiac arrest

D) All of the above

42

Which of the following is a protocol in the Emergency Action Plan (EAP) of a waterpark?

A) Assist with in-service training.

B) Monitor the chemistry of the pool water.

C) Inspect the baggage of patrons.

D) Stop the slide dispatch.

43

Waterfront facilities open to the public have lifeguards to ensure a swimmer's safety. There are some cases that a lifeguard will guard the entire facility.

Which of the following refers to the action of the lifeguard when a swimmer in distress is 100 ft away from the designated swimming area?

A) Take the time to observe the swimmer

B) Call your buddy and approach together

C) Start the rescue after you verified the possibility of drowning

D) Initiate the facility EAP and use the available rowboat to rescue the distressed swimmer

44

The Safe Swim Defense Plan allows a facility
and the swimmers to know the restrictions to
be followed. The requirements are also
present in the Safe Swim Defense Plan.

Which of the following refers to the
maximum recommended depth when
swimming in clear water?

A) 8 feet
B) 12 feet
C) 16 feet
D) 20 feet

SECTION 5

#	Answer	Topic	Subtopic	#	Answer	Topic	Subtopic	#	Answer	Topic	Subtopic	#	Answer	Topic	Subtopic
1	A	TB	SB3	12	B	TB	SB4	23	D	TB	SB3	34	D	TA	SA2
2	A	TA	SA2	13	B	TB	SB3	24	D	TB	SB2	35	C	TA	SA2
3	C	TA	SA3	14	A	TB	SB4	25	A	TB	SB2	36	D	TA	SA2
4	A	TA	SA2	15	C	TA	SA3	26	A	TB	SB4	37	B	TB	SB3
5	D	TB	SB3	16	B	TB	SB2	27	A	TA	SA2	38	D	TA	SA3
6	A	TB	SB2	17	D	TA	SA3	28	C	TA	SA3	39	C	TB	SB3
7	C	TA	SA2	18	C	TB	SB2	29	D	TB	SB4	40	B	TA	SA3
8	D	TA	SA1	19	A	TA	SA2	30	A	TA	SA2	41	D	TA	SA3
9	C	TB	SB4	20	B	TA	SA3	31	D	TB	SB3	42	D	TB	SB4
10	B	TB	SB4	21	B	TA	SA2	32	B	TB	SB3	43	D	TB	SB4
11	A	TA	SA3	22	B	TA	SA3	33	B	TA	SA2	44	B	TB	SB3

Topics & Subtopics

Code	Description	Code	Description
SA1	Lifeguarding Skills	SB3	Waterfront Skills
SA2	Professional Rescuer and First Aid	SB4	Waterpark Skills
SA3	Cardiopulmonary Resuscitation (CPR)	TA	Lifeguarding
SB2	Shallow Water Lifeguarding Skills	TB	Water Skills

CONTINUE ▶

TEST DIRECTION

Read the questions carefully and then choose the ONE best answer to each question.

Be sure to allocate your time carefully so you are able to complete the entire test within the testing session. You may go back and review your answers at any time.

You may use any available space in your test booklet for scratch work.

Questions in this booklet are not actual test questions but they are the samples for commonly asked questions.

This test aims to cover all topics which may appear on the actual test. However some topics may not be covered.

Studying this booklet will be preparing you for the actual test. It will not guarantee improving your test score but it will help you pass your exam on the first attempt.

Some useful tips for answering multiple choice questions;

- Start with the questions that you can easily answer.

- Underline the keywords in the question.

- Be sure to read all the choices given.

- Watch for keywords such as NOT, always, only, all, never, completely.

- Do not forget to answer every question.

CONTINUE ▶

1

Jumping feet first into the water must always contain the safety of the individual. It is recommended that basic diving such as this is to be done in more clear water to avoid any repercussions.

Which of the following refers to the bare minimum depth when jumping feet-first into the water?

A) Head-deep

B) Shoulder-deep

C) Chest-deep

D) Waist-deep

2

It is critical that a CPR is not interrupted for a long time since it may lead to death. The lack of action in the lungs may cause the next CPR attempt to take more than the appropriate time.

Which of the following refers to the amount of time that can be allowed during an interruption in chest compressions?

A) Less than 2 seconds

B) Less than 5 seconds

C) Less than 10 seconds

D) Interruptions are not allowed

3

An unconscious victim refers to a victim that is not aware of the surroundings. The victim can also be breathing or not breathing.

Which of the following refers to the techniques that are not suitable for moving an unconscious victim?

A) Four-handed seat carry

B) Two-man carry

C) Chair-seated carry

D) Improvised stretcher

4

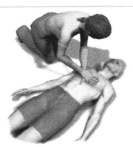

An unconscious individual was found lying on the ground. The scene is safe, but a CPR may be needed since the person is assessed to be not breathing.

Which of the following refers to the proper scenario that should happen after the assessment?

A) Check airway

B) Call for help

C) Start CPR

D) Check pulse

5

A fracture is a type of broken bone that may result in internal injuries like bleeding. It is recommended to seek medical attention immediately to heal the broken bone.

Which of the following refers to the accepted treatment for a femur or thigh fracture?

A) Remove and carry the victim away

B) Bind the legs by a soft cloth

C) This type of fracture is best handled by a traction splint applied by those with special training

D) The fracture has to be left until the bleeding stopped

6

A victim who is laying on the ground must be checked for pulse and breathing.

Which of the following refers to the treatment that must be followed for a victim whose life-threatening condition is "not breathing"?

A) Start compressions

B) Start CPR immediately

C) Give 20 rescue breaths and check the pulse

D) You should follow the steps for rescue breathing

7

Airway obstruction is the event that transpires when a foreign or artificial object blocks the breathing channel of a victim.

Which of the following refers to a sign of severe airway obstruction?

A) Wheezing

B) Light coughing

C) High pitched inhalation noise

D) None of the above

8

An **AED** is a tool that helps revive a patient who is not breathing or has an unstable heart rhythm.

Which of the following refers to the proper steps for operating an AED?

A) Power on the AED, attach the electode pads, analyze the rhythm, clear the individual, and deliver a shock

B) Power on the AED, attach the electode pads, deliver a shock, clear the individual, and analyze the rhythm

C) Attach the electode pads, power on the AED, deliver a shock, clear the individual, and analyze the rhythm

D) Attach the electode pads, power on the AED, analyze the rhythm, clear the individual, and deliver a shock

9

Turbid waters refers to water that is cloudy or full of muddy particles. They are usually deep and unclear which does not conform to safety when swimming.

Which of the following refers to the recommended water depth when swimming in turbid water according to Safe Swim Defense?

A) 5 ft

B) 7 ft

C) 8 ft

D) 10 ft

10

An acronym is a word or name formed as an abbreviation from the initial components of a phrase or a word, usually individual letters such as EMS (Emergency Medical Services)

Which of the following lifeguard acronym is not defined correctly?

A) AV; Atrioventricular Node

B) RWI; Recreational Water Illnesses

C) RID; Recognize Intrusion Distraction

D) HAINES; High Arm In Endangered Sport

11

CPR, or **Cardiopulmonary Resuscitation**, is a rescue method invented for life rescue and basic life-saving. The method includes breathing and compression techniques necessary to keep the person breathing.

Which of the following is the ratio of breaths to compressions if two rescuers are performing CPR on a 10-month old baby?

A) 15 compressions: 3 breaths

B) 15 compressions: 2 breaths

C) 30 compressions: 2 breaths

D) 10 compressions: 2 breaths

12

Frostbite usually occurs on the skin of a victim that is exposed to too much cold. The skin can become different in color as compared to the natural skin tone.

Which of the following refers to a true statement for treating frostbite?

A) Rub the area where there is frostbite to restore circulation

B) Wrap thick clothes around the frostbitten area to ease the pain

C) When you press on the skin of an area with frostbite, it will form an indentation.

D) Remove any tight clothing or jewelry from an area that has frostbite until the arrival of EMS.

13

A rescuer must determine that a person or victim requires a CPR at the least possible time. It is recommended that CPR be given within 10 seconds upon identification of the need for the procedure.

Which of the following hold true for the statement "CPR should be performed on an unconscious person who is unresponsive"?

A) The statement is true.

B) The statement is false.

C) The statement is false only for some cases.

D) The statement is unclear.

14

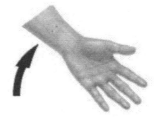

A poisonous snakebite can result in death if not treated carefully and immediately. There are cases that the victim dies in a very short amount of time.

Which of the following holds true for the statement, "The victim of a poisonous snake bite is not at risk for getting rabies"?

A) The statement is false.

B) The statement is unclear.

C) The statement is true only for some cases.

D) The statement is true.

15

Emergency Medical Service (EMS) system is a series of emergency services, like paramedic and ambulance services. It is used to treat injuries and illnesses that require immediate attention.

When an EMS is needed?

A) After calling 911

B) After providing CPR

C) Before providing CPR

D) After AED has been operated

CONTINUE ▶

16

A lifeguard's primary duty is the safety of the swimmers, especially in bad weather conditions. A lightning flash or thunder may indicate bad weather conditions.

Which of the following refers to the time frame that a lifeguard needs to allow swimmers after the last light flash or thunder to leave the shelter?

A) 20 minutes

B) 30 minutes

C) 45 minutes

D) 1 hour

17

The Chain of Survival is composed of the necessary means to save a life. It is important that the chain should not be broken to be able to save the life in the best possible scenario.

Which of the following is not one of the steps of the Chain of Survival?

A) Early CPR

B) Rapid defibrillation

C) Advanced airway placement

D) Basic and advanced emergency medical services

18

Before doing a CPR, it is necessary to immediately check for injuries regarding the head, neck or spine. It may largely affect the procedure and produce further complications.

Which of the following refers to the method to use to open the airway if there is a suspected head or neck injury?

A) Head tilt-chin lift

B) Jaw crush

C) Heilich maneuver

D) Head crush

19

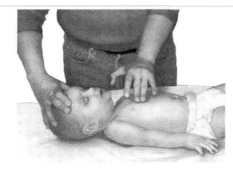

An infant is not breathing but the pulse is still present.

If you decide to do rescue breathing, which of following refers to the interval that breath should be provided?

A) Every 3-5 seconds

B) Every 4-6 seconds

C) Every 5-8 seconds

D) Every 8-10 seconds

CONTINUE ▶

20

A sprained ankle is possibly a torn or stretched ligament in the ankle region. A sprain may have been caused by an awkward landing, twisting, or turning of the ankle.

Which of the following refers to the first aid to be given to a person who has a sprained ankle?

A) Take your shoe off and check for swelling

B) Let the victim walk over to test the extent of the sprain

C) Take your shoe off, apply bandage, apply hot compress

D) Keep the shoe on, apply an ankle bandage for support, elevate and apply cold towels

21

A pulse check helps the rescuer determine the state of the heart rhythm of a patient.

Which of the following refers to the artery to be used for attempting a pulse check for a child who is between the age of 1-13 years old?

A) Ulnar artery

B) Brachial artery

C) Carotid or femoral artery

D) None of the above

22

If the rescuer is unsure of what to do for a victim, it is necessary to act on his capability. Moving a victim can cause either help or harm.

Which of the following hold true in moving a victim?

A) A victim should never be moved

B) A victim can only be moved by licensed professionals

C) In the recovery position, the top leg props up the body with the knee.

D) The recovery position places the mouth of the victim upward to allow them to breathe.

23

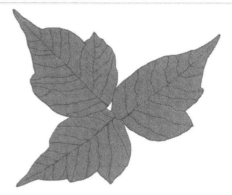

Poison ivy is a type of plant that causes induced dermatitis. It shows itching, irritation, and rashes in the skin.

Which of the following refers to the method of preliminary cure for poison ivy contact?

A) Let the itchiness fade away.
B) Spray the area with alcohol then wipe it clean.
C) Rub the area gently until the rashes disappear.
D) Rinse the effected area immediately with soap and water.

24

Upon the performance of CPR, the rescuer needs to determine the pulse and breathing of the patient. The standard steps are to be followed to ensure a higher chance of successfully performing the operation.

Which of the following refers to the 'C' in the C-A-B for CPR?

A) Clotting
B) Compression
C) Clearance
D) Current

25

During a CPR, the method can be tiring as it requires the technique to be executed well.

Which of the following refers to the frequency of switching when performing a CPR?

A) Every 5 cycles
B) Every 10 cycles
C) Every 15 cycles
D) Every 25 cycles

The waterfront, or pool, is usually separated by sizes. The larger ones are allocated more lifeguards than the smaller and shallower ones for the kids.

Which of the following refers to the action that should be taken when a lifeguard witnesses a swimmer in his zone grasping his chest and submerging in the water?

A) Call 911 immediately
B) Exercise your duty to act and perform the appropriate rescue
C) Take the time to see if there are other rescuers
D) Watch until the person is deeply submerged

A waterfront area must be designed with safety in mind apart from functionality and aestheticism. With regards to the lifeguard, it is required that they can oversee the area.

Which of the following refers to the action that must be taken if you cannot see some of the swimmers at one side of the swimming area from your station because of the glare from the afternoon sun?

A) Immediately report to your superiors
B) Request sunglasses and eye protection
C) Stay covered in the lifeguaard house and do not ccome out
D) Immediately adjust your position until you can see your entire zone

28

The Safe Swim Defense Plan is a standard plan to be recognized within a swimming institution. The Safe Swim Defense Plan will serve as a guide to run the swimming facility.

Which of the following refers to the number of directors needed and required under the Safe Swim Defense Plan?

A) 1

B) 3

C) 4

D) 7

29

A **buddy check** is made for checking equipment or status of another individual in your team. It is to ensure the stability of the team as well as the capability to attend to an emergency.

Which of the following refers to the primary purpose of the buddy check?

A) Remind participants to remain near their buddy so they can lend assistance

B) Activate the emergency response system

C) Determine activity of the lifeguard

D) Resist temptations while at work

30

A **pulse** is a heart rate measurement that describes the palpitation count of the heart. It is an essential method of observing a patient or victim that is to be rescued.

Which of the following refers to the best place to check for an infant's pulse?

A) The leg artery in the upper leg
B) The brachial artery in the upper arm
C) The carotid artery on the side of the neck
D) The radial artery on the pinky side of the wrist

31

Airway obstruction can be considered mild or severe depending on the symptoms of the victim. Identifying the type of airway obstruction will help the rescuer to decide for the next step on how to save the victim.

Which of the following refers to the action that the rescuer should do for a victim with a mild airway obstruction?

A) Try to remove the obstruction
B) Perform CPR and check breathing
C) Stay with the victim and monitor him
D) Apply short compressions to force out the obstruction

32

Rescue breathing, standard compression, and checking the breathing pattern of the victim are the main components of the CPR procedure.

Which of the following refers to the compression to breathing ratio when doing CPR?

A) 15 compressions to 2 breaths
B) 15 compressions to 3 breaths
C) 30 compressions to 1 breath
D) 30 compressions to 2 breaths

33

In CPR, it is necessary to be fast. An individual in cardiac arrest cannot wait for an ambulance and may lead to a "dead on arrival" case.

Which of the following refers to the first step when starting a CPR?

A) Chest compressions

B) Rescue breathing

C) Tapping the victim to be conscious

D) Relax and call for help in less than a minute

34

Airway obstruction refers to the inability of the victim to utilize his airway for breathing. It is a standard procedure to check for the airway clearance.

Which of the following refers to the signs of airway obstruction?

A) Shortness of breath

B) Inability for speech

C) High-pitch noise after exhaling

D) All of the above

35

Different depths of the pool may allow different methods of entry. If you are considering to dive, you may start at depths that are at 1.5 times your height.

Which of the following refers to the method of entry when entering the water from an elevated guard chair (greater than 3 feet)?

A) Run-and-dive

B) Compact jump

C) Backflip jump

D) Running jump

The swimmers around the pool are subject to reminders for safety before being allowed to enter the area. The swimmers are also liable for their safety.

Which of the following refers to the proper actions that should be taken by a lifeguard after the emergency action plan has been activated due to a possible cardiac arrest in the water?

A) Remove the victim from the water and call 911

B) Remove the victim from the water and prepare to begin CPR/AE

C) Remove the victim from the water and start planning

D) Call the victim to move on the side of the pool then act

SECTION 6

#	Answer	Topic	Subtopic	#	Answer	Topic	Subtopic	#	Answer	Topic	Subtopic	#	Answer	Topic	Subtopic
1	C	TB	SB3	10	D	TA	SA1	19	A	TA	SA2	28	A	TB	SB4
2	C	TA	SA3	11	B	TA	SA3	20	D	TA	SA2	29	A	TB	SB4
3	A	TA	SA1	12	D	TA	SA2	21	C	TA	SA2	30	B	TA	SA2
4	B	TA	SA2	13	B	TA	SA3	22	C	TA	SA1	31	C	TA	SA3
5	C	TA	SA2	14	D	TA	SA2	23	D	TA	SA2	32	D	TA	SA3
6	D	TA	SA3	15	C	TA	SA1	24	B	TA	SA3	33	A	TA	SA3
7	C	TA	SA3	16	B	TB	SB3	25	A	TA	SA3	34	A	TA	SA2
8	A	TA	SA2	17	C	TA	SA2	26	B	TB	SB4	35	B	TB	SB4
9	B	TB	SB2	18	B	TA	SA3	27	D	TB	SB4	36	B	TB	SB4

Topics & Subtopics

Code	Description	Code	Description
SA1	Lifeguarding Skills	SB3	Waterfront Skills
SA2	Professional Rescuer and First Aid	SB4	Waterpark Skills
SA3	Cardiopulmonary Resuscitation (CPR)	TA	Lifeguarding
SB2	Shallow Water Lifeguarding Skills	TB	Water Skills

CONTINUE ▶

Made in the USA
Columbia, SC
02 June 2022

61263715R00057